10/06
20–

I See a Pattern, What Can I Learn?

Tracy Kompelien

Consulting Editors, Diane Craig, M.A./Reading Specialist
and Susan Kosel, M.A. Education

Published by ABDO Publishing Company, 4940 Viking Drive, Edina, Minnesota 55435.

Printed in the United States.

Credits
Edited by: Pam Price
Curriculum Coordinator: Nancy Tuminelly
Cover and Interior Design and Production: Mighty Media
Photo Credits: AbleStock, ShutterStock, Wewerka Photography

Library of Congress Cataloging-in-Publication Data

Kompelien, Tracy, 1975-
    I see a pattern, what can I learn? / Tracy Kompelien
       p. cm. -- (Math made fun)
    ISBN 10 1-59928-533-9 (hardcover)
    ISBN 10 1-59928-534-7 (paperback)

    ISBN 13 978-1-59928-533-7 (hardcover)
    ISBN 13 978-1-59928-534-4 (paperback)
    1. Pattern perception--Juvenile literature. I. Title. II. Series.

BF294.K66 2006
515'.24--dc22

                                                                    2006012560

SandCastle Level: Transitional

SandCastle™ books are created by a professional team of educators, reading specialists, and content developers around five essential components—phonemic awareness, phonics, vocabulary, text comprehension, and fluency—to assist young readers as they develop reading skills and strategies and increase their general knowledge. All books are written, reviewed, and leveled for guided reading, early reading intervention, and Accelerated Reader® programs for use in shared, guided, and independent reading and writing activities to support a balanced approach to literacy instruction. The SandCastle™ series has four levels that correspond to early literacy development. The levels help teachers and parents select appropriate books for young readers.

Emerging Readers
(no flags)

Beginning Readers
(1 flag)

Transitional Readers
(2 flags)

Fluent Readers
(3 flags)

These levels are meant only as a guide. All levels are subject to change.

A pattern

occurs when one or more characteristics repeat according to a certain rule.

Words used to describe patterns:
alternate
color
repeat
shape
size

three
3

After each green slice comes an orange slice. This tells me that this color pattern repeats in twos.

This is orange and this is green. Alternating the two objects creates a color pattern.

This is a pattern in threes. I know this because the three objects repeat themselves.

The is a different shape from the and the . Repeating the shapes creates a shape pattern.

The small and large bananas alternate to make a size pattern.

The and the make up a pattern of different sizes.

I See a Pattern, What Can I Learn?

Patty uses patterns
when she is able.
She uses one
to set the table.
She alternates fork,
plate, knife, spoon,
fork, plate, knife, spoon.

twelve
12

Patty's dad has
a special tie.
Its colorful pattern
makes him a classy guy!

fourteen

14

Patty wears
this dress to school.
The pattern of flowers
is pretty cool!

Seeing Patterns Every Day!

When you make a necklace, it is fun to put the beads in a pattern.

I strung two dark beads and two light beads, and then I repeated the pattern.

eighteen
18

Can you see any patterns in your closet?

In my closet, I see patterns of color and shape. I can even order my clothes in a pattern of size. Can you?

twenty
20

Some socks have color patterns or shape patterns. Some have both!

The colors on my socks alternate and create patterns!

twenty-two

22

There are color, shape, and size patterns everywhere we go. Can you see any patterns at the grocery store?

Glossary

alternate – to change from one to the other over and over.

color – a combination of hue, lightness, brightness, and saturation.

repeat – to say or do something again.

shape – the form or outline of an object.

size – the measure of how big or small something is.